WILD BIRD GUIDES

Black-capped Chickadee

WILD BIRD GUIDES

Black-capped Chickadee

Susan M. Smith

STACKPOLE
BOOKS

For Doris

Published by
STACKPOLE BOOKS
5067 Ritter Road
Mechanicsburg, PA 17055

Printed in Hong Kong

10 9   8   7   6   5   4   3   2   1

First edition

Cover design by Tracy Patterson

Cover photo by Bill Marchel

Library of Congress Cataloging-in-Publication Data

Smith, Susan M., 1942–
      Black-capped chickadee / Susan M. Smith.
          p.   cm.—(Wild bird guides)
      Includes bibliographical references (p.).
      ISBN 0-8117-2686-X (pb)
      1. Black-capped chickadee. I. Title. II. Series.
QL696.P2615S55   1997
598.8'24—dc20
                                            96-24070
                                            CIP

Contents

General
Natural History

Chickadees are among the most familiar and beloved of birds. With their acrobatic maneuvers and inquisitive behavior, they are always a joy to watch. The Black-capped Chickadee is easily recognized by its distinctive dark cap and bib, which set off the paler cheeks. Chickadees seem to be in almost constant motion as they go about their daily business. They are extremely agile, often hanging upside down as they forage for food. They are among the few species that can actually be trained to eat food out of a person's hand.

Chickadees and their relatives belong to the family Paridae and are sometimes called parids. The Blue Tit is a parid that lives in Europe. Even though very different from North American chickadees, it still shows the same basic pattern of pale cheeks and somewhat darker cap and bib. Parids are found over much of the world, including most of North America, as well as Europe, Asia, and Africa.

Seven species of chickadees inhabit North America. Of these, the Black-capped Chickadee has the broadest range, from Alaska and much of Canada south to California and the Appalachians and from the Pacific to the Atlantic Ocean. The range includes Prince Edward Island, Newfoundland, and Nova Scotia in the Atlantic and Queen Charlotte Island and Vancouver Island in the Pacific.

Black-capped Chickadees, like other chickadee species, are tiny birds, weighing 10 to 14 grams, or between $1/3$ and $1/2$ ounce. Yet they are seldom afraid to approach much bigger birds. A chickadee is not scared away by the presence of Evening Grosbeaks at a feeder, for example, even though a grosbeak weighs more than four times as much as a chickadee.

Typical Black-capped Chickadees have white cheeks contrasting with a black cap and bib. The back is usually some shade of greenish gray, although it is somewhat warmer in color in certain parts of their range. They are white below, and their sides and flanks are washed with warm buff. The feathers of the wings and tail are dark gray with paler edges. Males and females are—to human eyes at least—essentially identical in appearance, and young chickadees have the same basic pattern found in older birds.

Sometimes chickadees have unusual color patterns. Most unusually colored birds are partially albino—that is, they have abnormal amounts of white on their feathers. This chickadee's white tail represents one of the most common forms of albinism. Most likely such chickadees have had a narrow escape from a predator. The chickadee managed to fly away, leaving the predator holding nothing but a bunch of tail feathers. But having had all of the tail feathers torn out at once damaged the bird's ability to produce normal gray pigment, and the replacement tail feathers, lacking this pigment, appear white.

Some years ago, it was thought that the Eurasian Willow Tit, shown here, and the North American Black-capped Chickadee were representatives of the same species. Certainly they look a lot alike. However, there are consistent plumage and behavioral differences, and recent biochemical data confirm that these are, in fact, two different species.

The Carolina Chickadee (left) of the southeastern United States is the North American species that most closely resembles the Black-capped Chickadee. The Carolina Chickadee has less white on the wings, however, especially on the greater wing coverts, the relatively short feathers near the bend, or shoulder, of the wing. By contrast, these wing coverts in the Black-capped Chickadee are broadly edged with white. Another visual difference is that the lower edge of the bib in Black-capped Chickadees tends to be uneven, giving at times almost a scaled appearance, whereas the division between the bib and pale underparts in Carolina Chickadees is usually more of a neat, straight line. Finally, the whistled song varies markedly. That of most Black-capped Chickadees is a relatively simple two- or three-note *fee-bee* or *fee-beeyee*, whereas a typical Carolina Chickadee song has four notes: *fee-bee, fee-bay.*

The Mountain Chickadee is another relative that resembles the Black-capped Chickadee quite closely. This species, however, has the black of its cap broken by a white line extending from the bill to well behind the eye; in addition, the sides and flanks are usually gray, although in some populations (for example, those in certain regions in the Great Basin) the sides and flanks are more buffy, thus more strongly resembling those of Black-capped Chickadees.

Black-capped Chickadees have been known to interbreed with both of these species, infrequently with the Mountain Chickadee, but somewhat more commonly with the Carolina Chickadee where the ranges of the two meet, in a line roughly from Kansas to New Jersey. Some scientists consider Black-capped and Carolina Chickadees to be forms of a single species, but there are consistent behavioral differences, and recent DNA analyses have shown considerable differences there as well. It seems probable that they are, in fact, separate species.

Besides these close relatives, several other bird species also resemble the Black-capped Chickadee to various degrees. Among these are the White-breasted Nuthatch, whose glossy black cap contrasts with pure white cheeks and gray back—all good chickadee field marks. Nuthatches lack the chickadees' black bib, however, and their tails are shorter and their bills longer than those of chickadees. In addition, nuthatches often walk headfirst down trees—a feat that chickadees, despite their agility, cannot manage. Certain warblers may also bear some resemblance to chickadees. Many have a similar high level of activity, and a few can have rather similar plumage as well. Perhaps the warbler most like chickadees in appearance is the male Blackpoll Warbler in breeding plumage, which can, from some angles, look remarkably like a chickadee. A closer look, however, reveals a streaked back, wing bars, and a white throat between a pair of black stripes.

The feathers making up chickadees' color patterns do not last forever; chickadees have to molt every one of their feathers each year. Molting takes place in late summer and early fall, usually starting after the adults have finished breeding. The worn feathers can make an adult in July look remarkably scruffy. This chickadee is molting, but the effects of the molt are hard to see, as it takes place gradually over a period of several weeks. This means that on any given day during the molt, a chickadee will have only a few less feathers than it would at other times of year. Chickadees molt during a time when temperatures are usually warm and food is plentiful. The quality of the new feathers is very important, since they must provide strong flight surfaces and keep the chickadees warm during the oncoming winter.

If a chickadee that is not molting has an accident and loses some feathers, it does not need to wait until the next molting period to grow them back. Instead, the lost feathers can be replaced right away. This chickadee has had a close call with a predator and has lost one of its tail feathers. A replacement feather will begin growing almost immediately, and in a few weeks the tail will be complete again.

Chickadees keep their feathers in good condition by frequent preening. This chickadee has just covered its bill with the secretions of its preen, or uropygial, gland, and is about to spread the oily, waxy substance carefully onto its feathers. The preen gland is located just above the base of the tail. Its secretions serve to keep the feathers flexible and make them more water-resistant.

Black-capped Chickadees are not very powerful fliers. Their flight is slightly undulating, with quite rapid wingbeats. They seldom go very far; most ordinary flights are less than 16 yards (15 meters) long. Normal chickadee flight speed is usually about 12 miles per hour (20 kilometers per hour). Infrequently they may hover for very short periods. When moving about after landing, chickadees typically hop rather than walk.

Given their relatively weak flight, it is no surprise that Black-capped Chickadees are nonmigratory, at least in the usual sense of the word. Certainly the same chickadees that breed in a given area will be resident there year-round. Nevertheless, every few years, Black-capped Chickadees may show evidence of a phenomenon known as an irruption, in which there is an upsurge in population. In irruption years, large numbers of chickadees, virtually all immature birds—the young of the year—may move southward in the fall. In many such years, at least some of these young birds may move back northward the following spring. However, these movements occur only every few years, and typically involve just a single age class—those birds hatched less than a year before the movements. True migration, by contrast, occurs every year and usually involves all age classes in the population.

Black-capped Chickadees live in an alternating social system: nonbreeding flocks in fall and winter, and monogamous, territorial breeding pairs during the spring and summer. Winter Black-capped Chickadee flocks are organized into distinct, linear peck orders, or dominance hierarchies. At this time of year, chickadees are hard to miss, as winter chickadee flocks frequently crowd noisily in to our backyard feeders.

In the spring, the flocks break up into pairs, and the behavior of chickadees changes drastically. Breeding chickadees can be very inconspicuous. Once territorial boundaries have been established, the resident chickadees are usually very quiet as they proceed with the business of nesting and rearing their offspring. Indeed, this change from noisy flocks to very quiet breeders leads some people to assume that the chickadees have all left in the spring, when active chickadee nests may actually be quite close by. After breeding is over, the juvenile chickadees will disperse from the place where they were hatched, then settle down some distance away and join the local adults to form new flocks for the coming winter.

Chickadees joining their first flocks in the fall will have an average life span of less than two years, yet several records exist of both male and females that lived until ten or eleven years of age, and the oldest known Black-capped Chickadee is a bird of unknown sex that, when last recovered, was at least twelve years and five months old.

Annual Cycle I Reproduction

Although chickadees spend the winter in flocks, there is strong evidence to suggest that these flocks are made up of pairs. In most areas, each chickadee flock, when first formed, contains an equal number of males and females. Moreover, close observation of the behavior of the flock members reveals that the birds spend more time associating with the other member of the pair than with the other birds in their flock and, given overwinter survival, such birds usually turn out to be mates the following spring. Remarkably, this is true not only for older birds, but also for birds that hatched the summer before the flock was formed. Thus the evidence strongly suggests that for all chickadees, regardless of age, pair formation is an essential part of flock formation.

Usually there will be at least some mortality over the course of a winter; it is rare for an entire chickadee flock to survive the winter intact. Occasionally new pairs are formed during the winter, but this is relatively uncommon— in most cases after winter mortality, the widowed bird, like the one shown here, does not get a new mate until spring. Regardless of when the pair forms, the actual selection of the mate is done by the females—the typical pattern in most animal species.

On warm spring days, chickadee flocks may begin to separate into pairs. Each pair will try to stake out a breeding territory within the flock's home range. Since chickadees normally begin breeding in their first spring—that is, at one year of age—every chickadee will attempt to get a mate and a territory. Often more than one pair will try to defend the same spot, and fighting may begin. Early on, this fighting is sporadic, depending largely on the weather. Loud and intense territorial encounters may occur when it is warm, yet if the next day is much colder, the same birds that were interacting so fiercely the day before may now be found feeding peacefully together once again. Gradually, as the spring progresses, these encounters increase until eventually the flocks break up for good.

In many areas, the number of chickadees alive at the end of the winter is greater than the number of breeding birds a given area can support, and so there is often not enough room for all the local birds to get breeding territories. When this occurs, the relative rank of the chickadees in the flock's peck order is all important: those pairs with the highest rankings will prevail, driving members of lower-ranked pairs away from the area. At this point, many such pairs split up and wander separately. When a chickadee has been excluded from the area where it lived during the winter, it often travels about in search of a territory owner that has just lost its mate. If lucky enough to find one of the appropriate sex, the chickadee may settle down and mate with the widowed bird.

Alternatively, chickadees that don't get breeding territories may stay where they spent the winter, but as nonterritorial birds known as summer floaters. Summer floaters usually range over three to six breeding territories, keeping pretty much out of the way of the resident chickadees. If one of the residents disappears over the summer, a floater may replace it and breed with its mate. Even if this does not occur, chickadees that have spent the summer as floaters will join the next winter's flocks at a much higher rank than that of incoming young birds, and thus have a good chance of breeding the following year. Oddly enough, this strategy is relatively rare; in many years, there may be no summer floaters at all, and even when there are floaters, they are few in number. Quite possibly the breeding chickadees permit the presence of summer floaters only in years when the local food supply is unusually high. All summer floaters thus far recorded have been birds that were members of local flocks the previous winter.

Although this driving away of lower-ranked birds may seem cruel, it is probably a very important process. First of all, it results in the strongest, most fit pairs being those that can breed. Moreover, it ensures that the chickadee pairs that do remain each have a sufficiently large territory to provide enough food for their young. In years when populations of important summer foods such as certain caterpillars are low, territorial pairs will be more likely to spend the energy to drive off floaters, thus guarding the limited food resources for their own offspring.

Even before flock breakup, chickadees begin exploring potential nest sites. This can happen very early—even in late January or early February in some locations—if a day is unusually warm and sunny. To begin with, these explorations are infrequent and are soon broken off. However, as the spring progresses, the explorations become more common and more intense.

Chickadees nest in cavities. By far the most common chickadee nest sites are in rotted portions of trees. Holes in stubs, snags, and rotted out knotholes are particularly favored. Where these sorts of locations are relatively scarce, chickadees may use old woodpecker holes or even nest boxes. Very rarely, Black-capped Chickadees may actually nest in a hole in the ground—a practice also known in some of their relatives, such as Mountain and Chestnut-backed Chickadees.

Wherever possible, chickadees dig out their own nest cavities, carrying off beakfuls of wood chips and scattering them some distance from the site. This practice prevents the buildup of wood chips directly below the cavity, which might attract the attention of predators. As in most North American chickadee species, both males and females excavate potential nest cavities. By the time a pair's breeding territory boundaries are firmly established, the chickadees have often explored and begun excavation in at least three to five different locations. Each member of the pair may have its own favorite spot, and a great deal of displaying may ensue, with each chickadee seemingly demonstrating the marvelous qualities of the cavity it has been working on, before the final choice is made.

Chickadee nest sites usually have side entrances. If the stub or branch is slanted at all, the entrance is often placed on the lower surface, giving extra protection from rain. Yet occasionally chickadees will nest in cavities whose only opening is at the top.

After the chickadees have selected the site and dug out the cavity to their satisfaction, the next step is to build a nest inside the chamber. There is one record of Black-capped Chickadees laying eggs in an unlined nest chamber, but this is very rare; most chickadees construct fairly complex nests before starting to lay their eggs. In Black-capped Chickadees, only the female builds the nest. This differs from the behavior of some close relatives, such as Mountain Chickadees, where both males and females participate in nest building. Female Black-capped Chickadees are often quite secretive while gathering material for their nests, although this can vary markedly from individual to individual. Usually material is gathered some distance from the nest site, and the female chickadee is very silent as she works.

To begin with, the female chooses quite coarse material like moss, pine needles, or perhaps strips of bark. With these she will build a thick foundation in the bottom of the nest cavity.

Sometimes the male accompanies his mate on her trips to get suitable material. I once saw a male triumphantly produce a caterpillar, which he proceeded to offer to his mate, but she had to reject it, as her bill was stuffed full of moss at the time.

Once she has finished building the foundation, the female will line the structure with softer material such as rabbit fur or the downy plant fibers attached to a variety of seeds. Nest construction usually takes three to four days, depending in part on the size of the cavity. Once the nest is finished, the chickadee often waits a day or two before beginning to lay eggs.

Female chickadees generally lay one egg per day, early in the morning, until the clutch is complete. Once the female has laid an egg, she emerges from the nest and spends the rest of the day with her mate, usually feeding quietly some distance away from their nest.

The male of the pair will catch food, such as caterpillars, and present it to his mate. Although his behavior is known as courtship feeding, it actually has little, if anything, to do with courtship itself. Such feeding usually begins very early in the spring, sometimes even before territorial boundaries have been established. It gradually increases in frequency, so that by late nest building it is pretty much at peak intensity; this intensity is then maintained throughout the egg-laying period. Laying a clutch of eggs is an enormous drain on the female's energy reserves. Sometimes the weight of a clutch of chickadee eggs can approach the weight of the female that laid them. Courtship feeding serves to sustain the female immediately before and during the strain of egg production.

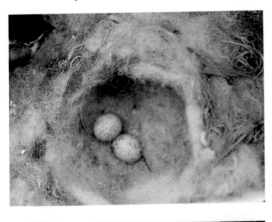

Chickadee eggs are white marked with many fine reddish brown spots and streaks, which are usually concentrated at the larger end of the egg. They are quite dull, rather than glossy, and average just under $2/3$ inch (15.2 millimeters) long and almost $1/2$ inch (12.2 millimeters) wide. Sometimes during egg laying, female Black-capped Chickadees may cover the eggs with nesting material when they leave the nest, so the nest appears empty. If a female is disturbed by something, however, she may leave in a hurry before she can cover her eggs.

After egg laying is completed, most Black-capped Chickadee nests contain six, seven, or eight eggs, although completed clutches of as few as one and as many as thirteen eggs have been recorded. The average clutch size for Black-capped Chickadees is just under seven eggs. Precisely how many eggs a particular female will lay can vary with a number of factors, including age (in most cases, older females tend to lay more eggs than do younger females), how late the nest was started (in general, the later the nest, the fewer the total eggs), and latitude (northern chickadee nests usually contain somewhat more eggs than southern nests).

The next step in the process is incubation. A female getting ready to start incubation develops a special area on her belly known as a brood patch. This is the area of her skin that will come in contact with the eggs. This area loses most of its feathers and temporarily develops an increase in blood vessels, so that the warmth carried by the chickadee's blood will be more easily transferred to her developing eggs. In Black-capped Chickadees, incubation is apparently done exclusively by females—certainly females are the ones that develop the most complete brood patches, and there are no records of males incubating. Males sometimes develop partial brood patches, however, although their function is as yet unknown. Incubation most commonly begins the day before the female lays the last egg of the clutch. Since eggs cannot begin to develop until they are incubated, this means that most of the eggs will begin developing at the same time, and the last egg will begin its development just twenty-four hours later. Such an incubation pattern usually results in all of the young hatching within twenty-four hours of each other; this is typical of virtually all chickadee nests early in the season.

There are great advantages to having this sort of incubation pattern. First of all, it limits the number of days the female must spend incubating the eggs, during which time she is vulnerable to certain nest predators, such as snakes or weasels. Also, the incubation process itself can be costly to females, especially during cold temperatures, when more energy must be used to heat the eggs; thus, the shorter the incubation period, the lower these potential costs to female chickadees. Finally, this incubation pattern ensures that all of the young in the brood will be essentially the same age and thus will leave the nest at approximately the same time. This can make care of fledged young a lot simpler. Nevertheless, there are occasions when female Black-capped Chickadees begin incubation well before the last egg is laid, usually when the eggs are laid late in the season—either after the parents have lost a set of offspring or, more rarely, when they have brought off one set of young successfully and decided to have a second set.

Why would chickadees change their incubation pattern in later nests? As time passes during the breeding season, the food supplies for young chickadees get less and less predictable, and the parents may not find much to bring to their nestlings. If incubation begins some time before egg laying is completed, the young will hatch in the order in which the eggs were laid. This will result in a set of young chickadees approximately one day apart in age. Say, for example, that a late nest has six eggs, yet it turns out that there is only enough food to bring off three young chickadees successfully. If incubation begins soon after the first egg is laid, then the young will be of different sizes, and the three oldest birds, being bigger and louder than the rest, will be the ones that get the most food. The youngest three will quickly starve. If this seems sad, consider the alternative: if all the young were the same age and begged for food at about the same level, then the parents would likely divide the food equally among all six nestlings, with the strong possibility that all six would starve.

Indeed, the fact that even in early nests, females begin incubation the day before they lay the last egg of the clutch means that female chickadees are hedging their bets, as the last egg will hatch about one day later than the rest. Four of these five nestlings already have their black cap feathers; the fifth, being a full day younger, has its cap feathers still covered with silvery feather casings. In years when there is slightly less food than usual, the youngest nestling in such a brood may die early, increasing the chances that its brothers and sisters will have enough food to survive.

An incubating female must eat; she therefore emerges from the nest at fairly regular intervals to search for food. This is often stimulated by the appearance of her mate, who periodically shows up at the nest site bringing her food. Sometimes he flies right to the nest entrance and gives her the food before she flies out; other times he may simply give a soft whistled call, and she responds by flying to him to be fed. After she has taken the food he has brought, the two birds feed quietly together for a few minutes before she returns to the nest. If the male stays away too long, the female will emerge from the nest and begin foraging alone; this usually brings her mate over to her in a hurry. While the female is on the eggs, her mate usually patrols the territory boundaries, returning frequently to the nest to bring her more food.

As soon as the female finishes eating, she returns to her nest to continue incubation. On average, incubating chickadees sit on their eggs for twenty to twenty-five minutes, then spend seven or eight minutes off the nest before going back in. Thus the females spend roughly three minutes on the eggs for every one minute away. While on the eggs, incubating females don't just sit there—they actually move around quite a bit, and often fiddle with the eggs. The result is that the eggs get turned frequently, which may be important for the normal development of the embryos.

Ordinarily, incubation in chickadees lasts twelve or thirteen days; then the eggs begin to hatch. Hatching can occur at any time of the day or night. Once an egg has hatched, the parents remove the eggshells from the nest. Usually they carry the shells some distance away, to be either discarded or, quite frequently, eaten, especially by the female, which had to produce the eggshell in the first place—a considerable drain on her calcium supplies.

These young chickadees are about a week old. When chickadees first hatch they are practically naked, having only six very small patches of soft grayish down on their upper surfaces. The young of Black-capped Chickadees are altricial, meaning that they are still very early in their development when they hatch. Newly hatched chickadees are very small, and their eyes are tightly shut. Their legs and wings are poorly developed, and practically the only behavior they are capable of at first is lifting up their heads in response to a particular call given by one of their parents, and gaping for food. The mouths of nestling chickadees are edged with bright yellow, which probably helps their parents aim the food in the relative darkness of the nest cavity. Until these young chickadees' feathers grow some more, they must depend on their mother for warmth. This means that even after the eggs have hatched, female chickadees must remain on their nests for considerable periods of time to protect their young from the cold.

Since most of the female's time is occupied brooding the newly hatched nestlings, the job of bringing food for all the hungry mouths falls on the male. For the first few days after the young have hatched, the male provides virtually all of the nestlings' food. Ordinarily, all of the food eaten by young chickadees is animal matter—mostly caterpillars. The nestlings must be fed several times an hour for as long as daylight persists.

These nestlings are about fourteen days old. Well-fed nestling chickadees grow rapidly. By about the fourth day after hatching, the first signs of dark spots are visible where their contour feathers (the kind of feathers that cover all adult birds) will grow. By about day seven, the nestlings' eyes begin to open; they are fully opened by day twelve. Shivering begins about day four and is well developed by day twelve, when the nestlings' contour feathers have broken through their sheaths at last. Thus by day twelve, the nestlings have finally grown a nice insulating feather coat to keep in the heat they generate by shivering. Now the nestlings are better able to regulate their own body temperature. Since they are no longer dependent on their mother for warmth, she is freed to take her turn at foraging for their food. Indeed, studies have shown that by day twelve or thirteen, males and females bring about equal amounts of food to the nestlings. The bigger the nestlings, the more food they need, and the parents must work very hard indeed to keep up with the demands of their voracious offspring.

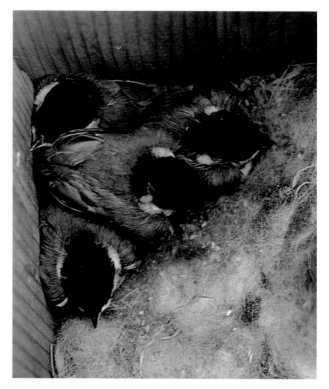

An inevitable result of all this feeding is considerable quantities of droppings. Nestling chickadees produce neat fecal packages wrapped in mucous envelopes, which the adult chickadees can easily pick up and remove, keeping the nest clean. The parent bird will fly some distance from the nest before dropping the package, thus avoiding telltale white splashes at the nest site, which could attract the attention of nest predators. Occasionally the parents may actually eat some of the fecal packages, especially those produced by very young nestlings. This is not as strange as it sounds; the newly hatched nestlings pass food through their developing digestive tracts very rapidly, and much nutrition remains unused. And the hard-working parents need all the energy they can get.

The time eventually comes for the young chickadees to leave the nest. This process, known as fledging, usually occurs about sixteen days after the young have hatched, although young chickadees may fledge earlier if their nest is disturbed. By day sixteen, the young chickadees' feathers are so well grown that they look very much like smallish adults, except for their short tails and traces of yellow at the corners of their mouths. Fledging usually takes place in the morning. Often the adults decrease the amount of food brought to the nest in the days leading up to the big event. A parent chickadee may then bring food to the nest but refuse to give it to the nestlings, thus helping to coax the hungry offspring out of the nest.

This young chickadee has just made its first flight. Flying is not difficult for young birds. Landing is another matter; managing to stop and keep one's balance while clinging onto a branch is an art that requires much practice. Thus many first flights end up on the ground. Once young chickadees have left the nest, they typically will not go back inside. Instead, after the last one has fledged, the entire family gathers together and moves off, away from the nest site. The family group—all of the fledglings plus both parents—may move some distance away from their nest, even on the first day. Both parents feed the young about equally, and a typical family group containing six to eight fledglings will consume an enormous quantity of caterpillars and other insects every day.

In the first few days after leaving the nest, the fledglings are completely dependent on their parents for food. Whenever they see an adult approaching, dependent chickadees give a loud, distinctive call that really does sound a lot like "Feed me! Feed me me!" The fledglings are also curious about their surroundings, however, and within a very few days of leaving the nest, they are already pecking at contrasting objects and beginning to catch some of their own food. This young chickadee has managed to obtain a green caterpillar all by itself. Gradually they catch a greater and greater proportion of their food, depending less and less on what their parents can provide—although the approach of either parent will continue to be greeted with ringing cries of "Feed me!" As the fledglings get older, the family groups may move farther and farther from their nest site. Family groups are even tolerated outside the boundaries of the pair's breeding territory—evidently adults that would be attacked as invaders when alone are often allowed safe passage if they are accompanied by a group of young chickadees all loudly demanding to be fed.

Chickadee family groups last only about three to four weeks, after which they break up and the young disperse. This can be a very sudden event—families that appear a tight and cohesive unit one day may be entirely dispersed the next morning. Exactly what causes this sudden dispersal of the young birds is as yet unclear. The adults don't chase them away—studies have shown no evidence of increased aggression toward the young. The dispersal is correlated with a decrease in food provisioning by the parents, but this is a gradual process and may be a result of decreased begging for

food by the young birds as they become independent, rather than being the cause of their leaving. Whatever the trigger for the dispersal, the young suddenly take off, each taking his or her own direction, and they leave their natal territory behind for good, often traveling quite

long distances—up to several miles—before finally settling down. One obvious beneficial consequence of such behavior is that the young birds, once they become old enough to breed, will have very little, if any, likelihood of mating with close relatives.

Dispersing young chickadees like this one travel quite rapidly for a period of several days. Dispersal directions are apparently random, and there seems to be no great difference between sexes in distance traveled. When the dispersal phase is over, the young birds settle down and join the local adults to start the formation of winter flocks. Once settled, most will remain in the same general area for the rest of their lives.

The pair bond formed by a young chickadee like this when it joins its first flock may persist for many years and might even last the lifetime of the individual. Birds that have bred together usually join the same flock in the fall and remain together all winter. However, it is not unheard of for intact pairs to break up, particularly when certain opportunities occur. In most such cases, a higher-ranked neighbor or flock mate has disappeared. When this happens, a chickadee may desert its mate to pair with the higher-ranked widowed bird, thus increasing its own rank in the process. Both males and females are known to engage in this form of social climbing.

Another kind of social climbing may also occur. Although scientists state that Black-capped Chickadees spend the spring and summer in monogamous pairs, monogamy, for Black-capped Chickadees, simply means that two birds, one male and one female, will cooperate in the production and raising of one or more broods of offspring. Nothing is implied one way or another about the very human concept of fidelity. In fact, matings with other birds, or extrapair copulations, occur fairly regularly among most birds, including chickadees. Interestingly, these extrapair copulations are by no means random events.

Behavioral observations of Black-capped Chickadees have shown that most are initiated by females and occur within the other male's territory. Moreover, in all of the known records of such matings, the female involved mated with a male that had ranked above her own mate during the previous winter. These behavioral records have recently been confirmed by DNA fingerprinting. Females typically are the ones that select mates; those females that end up paired with relatively low-ranked males may go elsewhere to obtain other, perhaps higher-quality, genes for their offspring. By contrast, female chickadees mated to top-ranked males evidently seldom, if ever, engage in extrapair copulations. Most extrapair copulations occur very early in the morning.

3

Annual Cycle II
Winter Flocks

It is late summer. All of the family groups have broken up, and the young hatched in the area have now dispersed. The adult chickadees that are still around are the local breeders, as well as any summer floaters there might have been during the breeding season. Joining these will be the incoming young chickadees, hatched some distance away, that disperse into the area. These young birds settle down, joining the older chickadees to form the winter flocks. Flock formation may take place over a period of several weeks. In western Massachusetts, where I live, this process usually starts in mid to late August and may continue until as late as early October in some years.

Pair formation is clearly an important part of flock formation, even for young chickadees. Within the flocks, members of the pairs tend to associate with each other more than with the rest of the flock, even when the next breeding season is many months away.

Several factors can affect how big local winter flocks will be. One of these is food supply—chickadee flocks tend to be larger in areas with lots of feeders. Another possible factor could be latitude; there is some evidence that chickadee flocks in northern areas may be somewhat larger than flocks in more southern locations. On the other hand, in areas where chickadees associate regularly with other species, such as kinglets, nuthatches, and woodpeckers, the chickadee flocks themselves tend to be smaller than in areas where such associations are rare. Chickadee flocks can have from two to as many as eighteen members. These extremes are rare, however; in most areas, flocks consist of six, eight, or ten members.

On a cold day in January, chickadees from different flocks may be found at a feeder with little, if any, aggression among them. These chickadees are from two different flocks. Yet chickadee flocks typically spend most of their time in distinct, well-defined areas called flock ranges. In late summer and early fall, chickadee flocks that meet at mutual boundaries of these ranges tend to have prolonged aggressive encounters, involving much loud calling and posturing, and at least some chasing, especially among the top-ranked birds of each flock. In the winter, however, the intensity of such encounters often diminishes greatly, especially if there is a concentrated food source, such as a feeder, near the boundary. If so, two or more flocks may visit the feeder simultaneously, with little overt aggression between the flocks. Black-capped Chickadee flock ranges can be anywhere from 20 or less acres to well over 50 acres in size (8.1 to 20.2 hectares). Sometimes two neighboring chickadee flocks may join together on a regular basis and forage as a single unit throughout the two flocks' combined ranges. Such compound flocks, as they are called, split up each evening, and each flock will sleep as a group within its own flock range; the compound flock may form again the next morning.

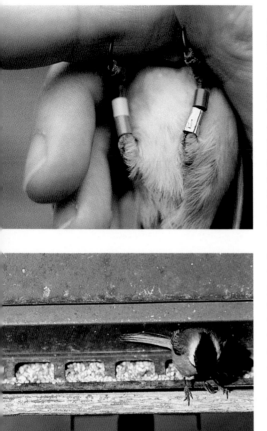

A great deal of interesting and complex social behavior goes on in winter chickadee flocks. In order to study this behavior, the researcher must be able to know which individual is which. This usually involves banding each member of the flock with a unique color combination on its legs, permitting individual identification in the field. The bands are extremely lightweight and pose no hazard to the birds. When individuals can be told apart, it becomes possible to see that chickadee flocks are stable groups of birds whose membership usually stays the same all winter. Moreover, the members of each flock are organized into distinct, linear peck orders, and the researcher can learn the relative rank of each member of the flock.

Chickadees rarely stay on a feeder to open a seed; ones that do are likely very high-ranked individuals. Several factors can affect the rank of a chickadee within its flock. One of these is sex; in general, within the winter flocks, males tend to be higher ranked than females (this will reverse in the breeding season). Another factor that affects relative rank is age; birds that are more than one year old usually rank higher than birds hatched the previous spring. Perhaps the size of the bird also has some effect; this has been shown in close relatives of chickadees in Europe, but not so far in Black-capped Chickadees. Finally, timing of joining the flock can also affect rank. Among the dispersing young birds joining local flocks, those that arrive earliest tend to have higher ranks than do later arrivals.

If males like this one are usually dominant over females in winter flocks, and there is a bad winter, such that half the flock does not make it, will there be only males left in the spring? Actually, it does not work out that way. Studies have shown that female overwinter survival is every bit as good as that of males, even in very severe winters. Does this mean that rank within the peck order has no effect on overwinter survival? No indeed. Between-sex rank is relatively unimportant, since females survive just as well as males, but by contrast, the relative ranking among chickadees within each sex matters a great deal. Thus for both males and females, chickadees that rank highest within their own sex survive significantly better than do lower-ranked birds of that sex. This is so regardless of age.

This chickadee ranks above all other females in her flock, and her mate ranks above all other males. This is not just a coincidence. In most chickadee flocks there is rank-matching among pair members—in other words, the top-ranked male's mate is the top-ranked female, the number two male is paired with the number two female, and so on throughout the flock. So an eight-member winter chickadee flock can be thought of not only as a linear peck order of eight individual chickadees, but also as a hierarchy of four chickadee pairs.

The alarm has sounded, and this chickadee is diving for cover. One of the major advantages chickadees get from joining together into flocks is that the more pairs of eyes there are, the more likely the birds are to spot predators quickly enough to escape their attacks. Extra eyes are helpful in foraging as well—the more pairs of eyes looking for things to eat, the more likely the whole flock will be to find food successfully.

Winter flocks of chickadees often associate, in a more or less regular way, with one or more other kinds of birds. Such groups are called mixed-species flocks. These associations are highly variable and can last just a few minutes or as long as weeks or even months. The species associating with chickadees in these mixed flocks vary with locality and season. In late summer, fall, and again in spring, several insectivorous species may join chickadee flocks. These include many warblers and vireos and, more rarely, other migrants, such as flycatchers. Black-capped Chickadees also frequently associate with other winter residents, including Downy, Hairy, and Red-bellied Woodpeckers; White-breasted and Red-breasted Nuthatches; Brown Creepers; and Golden-crowned and Ruby-crowned Kinglets.

Birds involved in these mixed-species flocks can be divided into leader and follower species. Chickadees are definitely leader species; most of the other kinds mentioned above are follower species, although Golden-crowned Kinglets may form their own equally independent flocks. Certain closer relatives may also be involved in mixed flocks with Black-capped Chickadees where their ranges overlap. These include Tufted Titmice and Chestnut-backed, Boreal, Mountain, and Carolina Chickadees.

Mixed-species flocks will also form some sort of peck order, often based more or less on the relative size of the individuals involved. A White-breasted Nuthatch at a feeder will rank above a Black-capped Chickadee, which in turn will rank above any kinglets in the group. Yet the chickadees' relatively low position in the peck orders of mixed flocks clearly doesn't put them at much of a disadvantage.

Studies have shown that mixed flocks are more likely to form in natural areas containing few or no feeders. Perhaps where feeders make food-finding relatively easy, other species do not need to depend on the extra eyes chickadees and titmice provide to search for food. One interesting thing is that the number of members in a winter flock remains relatively constant, regardless of how many species are represented. So a ten-member flock in a feederless area might consist of six chickadees, two nuthatches, a woodpecker, and a Brown Creeper; in a nearby area supplied with lots of extra food a flock might consist of ten chickadees. The result of this is that the average number of chickadees per flock will be higher in an area with pure flocks than it is in areas

where mixed flocks are common. This may be due in part to competition. Generally, the strongest competition will be between members of the same species, since their needs are essentially identical. If some of the eyes looking out for food and predators are provided by other species, chickadees may get the same benefits while experiencing less severe competition.

Under some circumstances, the flock structure of wintering chickadees may be very hard to decipher. This may give a superficial impression that the local chickadees are not in flocks at all, even in the middle of winter. Several factors can contribute to this apparent lack of cohesion. One is weather—chickadees tend to be more widely dispersed on warm, sunny winter days. The distribution of food supply within a flock range can also affect how closely united a flock appears to be; flocks in ranges where food is concentrated may appear more cohesive than those whose range contains more widely dispersed sorts of food. Individual differences also come into play here; certain chickadees tend to be somewhat more independent than others, and these may occasionally stray some distance from the rest of the flock or, alternatively, may stay put in a certain favorite spot, even when most of the rest of the flock has moved to a different portion of the flock's range.

In addition to all of the above, certain chickadees may be present that are particularly mobile. For example, older chickadees like this one, usually at or near the top of their flock's peck order, may occasionally wander far from their normal flock range. Such birds, called dominant wanderers, are always regular members of one particular flock. Both single birds and mated pairs may wander in this way. Although it is unknown what causes such birds to roam so far, at least one benefit of such behavior is clear: these birds can scout out concentrations of food in the areas surrounding their flock range, to which they can return during times of food shortage. The effects of this are relatively easy to see: isolated feeders may be visited by three, four, or even more flocks, especially in midwinter. These flocks were presumably each led to the feeder by their own dominant wanderers.

The winter floaters are another class of chickadees with unusually wide home ranges. These birds, like the one shown here, are young, unpaired chickadees that, under some circumstances, may respond to the death of a higher-ranked bird by settling into its flock and pairing with its mate, even in the middle of winter. These floaters usually move freely within three to five flock ranges, and each one has a position down near the bottom of the peck order of each of the flocks—always below every regular member of their sex. If a high-ranked member of a flock dies during the winter, it may be replaced by a floater. For example, if the top-ranked female in a flock of eight birds disappears, a winter floater may quickly settle into the flock and start associating closely with the widowed male. Once

paired with the top-ranked male, she will become the top-ranked female in the flock, suddenly able to chase away birds that, days before, could easily chase her off. The same thing can happen if it is a male that vanishes, so long as the bird that has disappeared was ranked highly in the flock's peck order.

The mate of this low-ranked female died a few weeks ago, but no winter floater has replaced him. Two factors seem to affect whether floaters will settle into winter flocks in the manner described above. One is the rank of the chickadee that vanishes—only high-ranked birds are replaced by floaters, whereas low-ranked openings in chickadee flocks remain unfilled all winter. The other factor seems to be the relative density of floaters; floaters seem much more likely to be able to settle into a flock when their density is relatively high. It is not too surprising that winter floaters don't settle into low-ranked openings; even if filling such openings means a small jump in rank, low-ranked pairs seldom get to breed locally. Remaining an unpaired floater for a bit longer may pay off if the floater can move into a higher-ranked slot later on, giving it a much better chance of becoming a breeder. Just why the density of floaters affects their chances of replacing high-ranked flock members that have vanished is not yet known, although perhaps most widowed birds are more likely to accept a replacement immediately if there is a clear choice of candidates for the position.

So-called migrants are a third class of highly mobile chickadees that may appear in the winter. Although Black-capped Chickadees do not undertake yearly long-distance migrations, movements do occur under some circumstances. Two kinds of movements can result in the influx of these migrants into a given area. First, severe conditions at high altitudes can force chickadees to move down to lower areas with milder conditions. Second, chickadees moving southward during irruptions must stay somewhere during the winter. In either case, these migrants evidently do not join local flocks; they have their own home ranges, which may overlap with two or more local flock ranges.

No wonder that in some areas wintering chickadees appear to have little organization into flocks! The exact membership of local winter flocks cannot possibly be worked out until each of these more mobile kinds of chickadees can be recognized individually first. Only then will it be possible to discern the actual, often complex social organization functioning among the chickadees wintering in any particular area.

4

Diet and Foraging

Chickadees absolutely have to eat—a lot—every day. They are warm-blooded, with a high metabolic rate, and keeping their temperatures up all day requires a great deal of fuel, especially in winter. Some people might think that on cold stormy days chickadees don't feed at all, but in fact, the worse the conditions, the more chickadees need to eat.

A spider is hidden in among these berries—but not well enough to escape being spotted by this chickadee. In catching the spider, the chickadee will likely use its most common foraging maneuver: gleaning. A gleaning chickadee simply stretches out its head, while perched, to pick up food items from any surface within reach.

Hanging is the second most common foraging maneuver used by Black-capped Chickadees. Chickadees and their relatives have unusually strong leg muscles, which permit them to hang upside down with ease.

Besides gleaning and hanging, chickadees can also use three other, less common, foraging techniques. One is to hover in midair to get at food items on the very tips of thin twigs.

Another is to use their bills to probe into hidden spots, such as curled leaves. Finally, they may use the behavior termed hawking, in which a bird flies out and catches food such as flying insects in midair.

The natural diet of Black-capped Chickadees is about 70 percent animal matter (largely insects and spiders) and 30 percent plant matter (seeds and berries). The precise proportions of these foods vary with the season, however. In winter the usual chickadee diet is about half animal and half plant material, whereas in the warmer months a much higher proportion of the chickadees' diet is animal matter, including a wide variety of insects, especially larval forms such as caterpillars.

Black-capped Chickadees eat many kinds of seeds. Milkweed seeds may be particularly favored in the fall. Other weed seeds frequently eaten by chickadees include those of goldenrods and ragweeds.

Sunflower seeds are especially nutritious, and chickadees are strongly attracted to them whether they are in natural settings or in feeders. These seeds have a high oil content, which makes them an important food source during the coldest days of winter.

Another important food source, where available, is the seeds from various kinds of rushes. Because these are often very tall, they remain uncovered by snow all winter and thus can be particularly important after severe snowstorms.

Conifer seeds are also extremely important to Black-capped Chickadees. These seeds are often highly nutritious. Moreover, in many conifer species, the cones may grow at widely dispersed points within a given tree, so each member of a chickadee flock can feed relatively undisturbed. In stormy weather, the foliage of coniferous trees can provide essential shelter for the foraging birds.

Berries are also an important part of the winter diet of chickadees. Large berries will be eaten on occasion, especially in severe cold, but smaller kinds, such as the wax-covered berries of poison ivy and bayberry, are usually far more important in the diet of Black-capped Chickadees.

Most of the animal matter eaten by chickadees consists of insects and spiders. Naturally, the kinds will depend on the season. During the warmer months, when insects can be active, mobile forms such as adult and larval insects, as well as various kinds of spiders, make up a very large part of the food chickadees eat.

Chickadees also need to eat insects and spiders during the cold of winter, even when it is far too cold for such creatures to be active, and they know where to look. Many kinds of insects and spiders spend the winter hidden in the bark of trees and other types of plants. These can be in the form of eggs, pupae, or even overwintering larvae and adults. They can also be hidden on the undersides of smaller twigs and branches, which may protect them from some bark foragers, such as woodpeckers, but doesn't give very much protection from birds that are as agile as Black-capped Chickadees.

This chickadee is searching for the larvae of wood-borer beetles. Although the larvae are not easy to catch, their large size makes them worth trying for, especially if their density is relatively high.

Animal fat, in any form, is an extremely important food for chickadees, particularly in cold weather. Ounce for ounce, fat provides more calories of stored energy than any other form of food. Many seeds have a high fat content, but overwintering insects and spiders contain relatively little fat. Thus chickadees are always on the lookout for more, especially during the cold winter months. Suet feeders are excellent sources of this necessary food. Moreover, they are not as artificial as one might think. If a chickadee flock finds a dead animal during the winter and the skin has been broken by scavengers, the chickadees will readily come down to eat the precious fat hidden underneath the animal's skin.

When a chickadee finds a piece of food, it seldom eats it on the spot; rather, it carries off the food to a safer location and eats it there. Safety could be in terms of protection from predators or, if the chickadee is fairly low in the flock's peck order, in terms of avoiding attention of greedy flock-mates as well.

Once a chickadee takes its food to a safe location, the food may need to be manipulated in some way before the chickadee can eat it. A chickadee will use its feet to hold down a sunflower seed so that it can pound open the shell with its bill. Animal food may also need to be manipulated in this way. A chickadee will usually remove the head, wings, and legs from any large insect it catches before

eating the rest. The chickadees' ability to use their feet in food manipulation is relatively unusual among perching birds.

Chickadees rarely come to the ground for food. Most of their foraging is done in vegetation some distance above the ground. Precisely where a particular chickadee will look for food depends on many different factors. Seasonal and local distribution of food is an obvious one; some areas may have an outbreak of a certain insect much relished by chickadees, or there might be a particularly rich berry or cone crop. Year-to-year variation is also a factor here; an area that has an outbreak of caterpillars that live only in bushes in one year may have none the next year, forcing chickadees to search for food in vegetation of other heights. In some years, hemlock cones will provide seeds in abundance, and chickadees will forage extensively in these trees; the next year there may be no new hemlock cones, and the chickadees must forage elsewhere.

Weather can also affect where chickadees spend time looking for food. Wind, in particular, has a strong effect on foraging location. On cold, windy days, chickadees forage much lower down, and often in denser vegetation, than they will on warmer, calmer days. This makes a great deal of sense. Wind can ruffle a chickadee's feathers, which can cause dangerous heat loss. A chickadee's feathers are most effective when the outer layer lies smooth and neat; any ruffling of the feathers creates breaks in this protection, letting body heat escape.

Another factor affecting where a particular chickadee forages is the rank of that chickadee within the flock's peck order. The highest-ranked individuals get to forage in the best spots, both in terms of quality and richness of food, and also in terms of relative safety from predators. Lower-ranked chickadees must therefore look for food elsewhere. A low-ranked chickadee, like the one shown here, may have to spend much of its time foraging in outer branches, where it is more exposed to predators. This effect of rank has been demonstrated convincingly by removal experiments; if the most dominant individuals are removed from a flock, the lower-ranked chickadees immediately start foraging where the dominants had been. When the removed birds are released back into the area, they take over once again, forcing the rest to go back to foraging in the poorer locations.

Caterpillar damage to leaves is an important foraging cue used by Black-capped Chickadees. This is not as simple as it might appear. Whether or not chickadees are attracted to various patterns of holes in leaves must depend in part on the kind of tree, since such holes may indicate good-tasting caterpillars in some tree species but bad-tasting caterpillars in others.

Chickadees are inquisitive birds, always ready to explore new objects in search of food. They are remarkably intelligent and learn quickly. Black-capped Chickadees feeding in flocks evidently keep a sharp eye on what their companions are doing, and how successful it is. If a chickadee sees another having success doing a particular activity in a certain location, it will probably do likewise. This kind of copying can permit any effective new technique to spread rapidly among the local chickadee population.

Besides food, water in some form also is essential for chickadees. Birdbaths can be very important to them, particularly in the summer, which is when small birds need water the most. During the hottest summer weather, chickadees must have regular access to water in order to survive.

Since chickadees must fly in even the hottest weather, and flying generates a great deal of heat, the greater the heat, the greater a chickadee's need for water. On very hot summer days, chickadees will pant in an attempt to cool down. Panting will work, but it also uses up a lot of water, so the chickadee must drink enough to avoid dehydration.

Chickadees also need water at other times of year. Some can be obtained from the food they eat. During the winter they may drink water dripping from icicles, as shown on page 38, or eat snow.

One fascinating aspect of chickadee foraging behavior is the fact that they frequently store food for future use. Such stores of food can be vital to the chickadee's survival in subsequent periods of severe weather. Most of the food items stored by chickadees are seeds, although they do sometimes store other sorts of food, even insects at times. Chickadees typically do some preparation of food before storing it; for example, they sometimes take off the shells of sunflower seeds and often remove at least the heads of insects. However, not all food to be stored needs such preparation; I once bought some suet that had been put through a meat grinder, resulting in masses of rice-sized pellets of the fat. When we put some out in our feeder, the chickadees set to work immediately, carrying off huge numbers of these pellets to hide away for the future.

Chickadees store food almost anywhere. The best sites are small niches or crevices where a seed or other food item can be tucked away out of sight, such as a crack in a stump or in the bark of a big tree. Knotholes are another good location, as are curled leaves or needle clusters, especially those on the undersides of relatively slender branches. Around human habitations, chickadees may also store food under shingles or other man-made locations providing the necessary small openings where such items can be hidden. Black-capped chickadees have even been known to store seeds in the ground.

Although chickadees may store food items at any time of year, by far the most common time for food storage is in the fall. In some cases, chickadees and their relatives can store prodigious quantities of food; Black-capped Chickadees have been known to store upward of a thousand seeds in a single day. Not surprisingly, chickadees and their relatives that live in more northerly regions, and will thus experience more severe winters, generally store more food items than do birds living in milder climates. In Norway, an average titmouse reportedly stores between fifty thousand and eighty thousand seeds in a single autumn.

Chickadees do not have one central place where they hide their food; rather, they hide each piece in a separate location. The advantage of this method is that if a competitor finds where a chickadee has stored food, that chickadee will be robbed of only one piece, rather than the entire hoard. Of course, the down side of this arrangement is that the bird that stored all those food items has to remember where each one is. Yet that is precisely what Black-capped Chickadees can do. This chickadee is about to retrieve a seed it stored in one of these wood-borer holes about two weeks ago. The bird will have no difficulty in finding the right hole. Chickadees can even remember the sites from which they have already removed their seeds, so they don't waste time searching for what they have already used. Indeed, studies have shown that chickadees can actually remember what they stored where—that is, they can remember the relative quality of each food item in each location. When they return, they tend to go first to those sites where the best-quality food has been stored.

All of this ability requires a quite amazing capacity for memory. In fact, it turns out that the spatial memory (memory regarding location) of chickadees and their relatives is far more developed than that of most other birds. A portion of the brain called the hippocampus is strongly involved in spatial memory. In chickadees and their relatives, this part of the brain is far larger than it is in birds that do not store any food. Incredibly, there is now evidence suggesting that in Black-capped Chickadees at least some portion of the hippocampal region of the brain may break down and be renewed every year, usually just before the fall peak of food storing. In this way, old memory patterns of last year's locations, no longer useful to the bird, will be lost, and the bird will grow a new set of hippocampal cells to be involved in the memory of this year's food storage locations.

In autumn, when most food storing occurs, chickadees are in flocks. Individuals that are about to store food are thus seldom really alone. This brings up the possibility of pilfering—one chickadee simply taking food items stored by another. Although pilfering does occur, it may not be as frequent as one might suppose. For one thing, chickadees are less likely to hide anything when others are particularly close; they may wait until they are farther away from their companions before storing their food. Also, the spatial memory of chickadees seems to work best for food they have stored themselves—if a chickadee sees another

hiding a food item but for some reason does not take it right away, its chances of remembering where it was hidden seem to be quite slim.

Chickadees may regularly retrieve seeds shortly after hiding them and then store them in new, possibly safer, locations. Chickadees have been shown experimentally to be able to find seeds stored at least one month previously, although it is likely that their memory covers even longer time spans. Certain Eurasian parids have been found in midwinter eating seeds that have not been available naturally for several months, strongly suggesting that the seeds they were eating had to have been stored a lot more than just one month before.

Chickadees and their relatives have intelligence, agility, curiosity, and amazing neurological capabilities, all of which make them particularly efficient foragers. We are only beginning to learn about some of the remarkable adaptations that aid them in their never-ending search for food.

Social Behavior
and Communication

Social behavior in Black-capped Chickadees is varied and intriguing and necessarily changes over the course of a year, as their social organization passes from the complexities of flock living during the fall and winter through to the highly territorial, monogamous breeding pairs of the spring and summer.

At the beginning of the breeding season, territorial breeding pairs may engage in vigorous boundary disputes with their neighbors. This chickadee is ducking out of the way as her mate chases off a member of a rival pair. Sometimes, especially in early spring, these disputes may involve three or even four pairs, and the action can be fast-paced and furious. Short chases are common in these encounters. So are supplanting attacks, in which one chickadee actively takes over the place where another was perched. Very rarely, these disputes may even escalate to the point where two birds will fly up together, grappling with their feet and attempting to peck one another. If they do lock feet, they may both fall to the ground, separating only after impact. Both males and females may participate in boundary disputes, with each bird calling loudly and chasing off invaders. Males virtually always take an active part in these disputes. Female behavior varies with the individual; some become just as involved as their mates, while others take a less active role.

One of the most commonly used vocalizations in these disputes is a complex one, often termed the gargle. The gargle is used frequently throughout the year by either sex in any aggressive situation. This vocalization is rather difficult to describe, as it varies widely, each individual having a repertoire of fifteen or so different versions. Gargles also vary both with location and with time. Thus, within a given year, gargles given by Black-capped Chickadees in one area may be very different from those given by chickadees a few miles away. And this year's gargles given by chickadees in one location may be quite different from last year's gargles in the same location. One fairly common gargle call of chickadees near my home in western Massachusetts might be written as *ch'dle-ee, ch'dle-ee.*

In the spring, another sort of encounter also starts to occur, this time within pairs. In the winter flocks, males are virtually always dominant over their mates. Once the pairs separate and establish the boundaries of their breeding territories, however, this relationship starts to change. The change is subtle and hard to document, especially as dominance interactions between the two birds are relatively rare at these times. Many authors, if they remark on this at all, simply report that the males lose their dominance over the females. However, careful observations show that, especially during the spring and early summer, females are the ones that win any aggressive interactions with their mates. They may even give gargle calls as they supplant their mates at favored food sources, perches, or other resources.

Another familiar sound often associated with spring territorial behavior of Black-capped Chickadees is their beautiful, whistled, loud *fee-bee*. This is given primarily by males. Although loud *fee-bees* can be heard at any time of the year, they are by far the most common in the spring. On warm spring days, males will use loud *fee-bees* to engage in prolonged vocal exchanges with their neighbors, especially early in the morning. In most Black-capped Chickadee populations, the loud *fee-bees* actually involve three notes. The first *(fee)* is highest, the second *(bee)* is lowest, and the third is sometimes very slightly higher in pitch than the second—*fee-beeyee* (or "hey sweetie," according to one researcher). A few relatively isolated populations, however, have different versions of this whistled vocalization. For example, Black-capped Chickadees in some parts of Washington give a string of whistled notes all about the same pitch: *fee, fee, fee, fee, fee*. Chickadees living on Martha's Vineyard also have quite different patterns of whistles that actually vary with location on the island. Regardless of pattern, in the loud vocal bouts heard in spring, an integral part of the interaction may involve variations in the pitches of one male's whistled notes and how these differ from those of the other male. These variations can signal changes in the intensity of such aggressive vocal exchanges.

Most bird vocalizations, especially those given by the group of birds known as songbirds (which includes chickadees and their relatives), usually fall into one of two categories: songs or calls. Songs are often relatively longer, more complex, and made up of purer tones; calls, by contrast, tend to be shorter, simpler, and often harsher in tone. True songs tend to be used primarily to attract mates and to fend off would-be rivals; calls can be used for a large number of functions, and birds often have a whole repertoire of different calls, each with a different meaning. Gargles and loud *fee-bees* each perform some of the functions of songs, and some scientists consider both to be songs of the Black-capped Chickadee.

Besides these two kinds of songs, several calls of chickadees are also strongly associated with the breeding season. One of these is the faint *fee-bee*. This sounds very much like the ringing song mentioned above, but the volume is much softer, and the context and message are quite different. Faint *fee-bees* are usually given during feeding interactions at or near the nest. This male chickadee, which has found a caterpillar to bring to his incubating mate, will give faint *fee-bees* as he approaches their nest. This will signal his arrival to her. Adults of both sexes may also give faint *fee-bees* when they bring food to their nestlings.

Another call given only during the breeding season is a very high, thin note, referred to by scientists as the variable *see*. This note, which can be given by either sex, is usually associated with mating itself. Mating in chickadees is accompanied by remarkably little display. Either member of the pair can initiate the process by giving a whole string of variable *sees;* its mate usually joins in. When the male approaches, in addition to the variable *sees,* he may give a special form of the gargle note. If the female is ready, she will begin to quiver her wings, and the pair then mates. Often one or both chickadees give variable *sees* during copulation. Afterward, the female may continue wing quivering for a few seconds, before beginning to preen. Then the two birds move off quietly together. Mating begins quite early in the breeding season and peaks during egg laying. Most mating occurs shortly after dawn.

Early in the spring, when the male begins courtship feeding, the female may receive his gift silently, or even with a short gargle. Courtship feeding will continue right through to the end of incubation, but as the season progresses, the female's behavior will gradually change. Especially during nest building, egg laying, and incubation, any female who sees her mate approaching will often give a vocalization called broken *dees*. This call is given exclusively by females and is always associated with courtship feeding. By the time the nest is being built, females usually accompany their broken *dees* with wing quivering as well. Any male hearing his mate give this call typically responds quickly by presenting her with a piece of food.

Soon after the nestlings hatch, their father will go off in search of food for them. When he returns to the nest, he will probably give a special call, termed the squawk. Evidently newly hatched Black-capped Chickadees seldom gape for food spontaneously, especially during their first forty-eight hours after hatching. Squawk calls, which can be given by either parent, are perhaps the most effective stimulus to elicit gaping for food by newly hatched nestling chickadees.

Sometimes all the activity around the nest can attract the attention of a predator. If either parent is caught inside the nest cavity by a potential predator, the threatened chickadee may put on a complex defensive display. The chickadee stands up as high as it can within the confined quarters of the nest cavity, with its neck stretched tall; then it suddenly brings its head down and forward, giving a loud hiss. At the same time, the chickadee spreads its wings out strongly so that they hit the sides of the nest cavity. This has been termed the snake display, as the sudden forward and downward head movement accompanied by the loud hissing sound bears an obvious resemblance to a striking snake. Squirrels, chipmunks, weasels, opossums, and raccoons, as well as snakes themselves, are all possible predators that attack chickadee nests and thus could elicit this display. Snake displays are given only if a chickadee is in a tight place, most often in the nest cavity itself, when threatened.

If a threat is encountered near, but outside of, the nest, one or both parents may give the nest-site distraction display, which is quite different. The chickadee slowly raises and lowers its fully extended wings, repeating this over and over. It spreads its tail and may bow repeatedly, turning from side to side. Although this display may be given by only one chickadee, of either sex, it is perhaps most often given by both parents at once. The sight of two chickadees courageously posturing with waving wings and flared tails is one not soon to be forgotten. Although this display is most often given by adults whose nest or newly fledged young are threatened, it can also be given by a chickadee whose mate is in danger.

Despite all of the potential threats, many chickadee nests are successful. When the young chickadees leave their nest, they will give a very characteristic call, the begging *dee,* whenever they detect an approaching adult. These calls, which sound a lot like "feed me! feed me me!" also sound quite a bit like the broken *dees* given by females during courtship feeding, although there are consistent subtle differences between the two. Interestingly, both of these calls are often associated with wing quivering, and each usually results in the caller's being fed. The young chickadees will continue to give begging *dees* until their family flock breaks up and they disperse from their natal territory.

Two other calls, the contact call and the flight, or restless, note, are given very commonly by Black-capped Chickadees of either sex throughout the year. Indeed, the contact call, a short, soft, fairly high *tseet,* is given almost incessantly by undisturbed chickadees and likely serves to keep chickadees informed about the location of others. Often during the daytime, chickadees will stop giving this call only if they are suddenly disturbed; the abrupt cessation of these sounds may itself serve to communicate alarm to any other chickadees within earshot.

Flight, or restless, notes are sometimes referred to as the "let's go" call. They are very similar to contact calls, but louder and given more rapidly. Flight notes are given primarily when a chickadee and its companion or companions are about to move off to a new location some distance away. Often they are given just before the pair or group moves off, but they also may frequently be given during flight itself.

If a Black-capped Chickadee sees a predator coming fast, it will stop moving as soon as possible, then give the high-intensity alarm call: a very high-pitched, thin call termed the high *zee.* Any chickadee hearing high *zee* notes may stay immobile for up to two minutes or even longer. Certain qualities of this call make it very hard to locate, so predators are unlikely to be drawn to the calling bird. Other small birds, like nuthatches, kinglets, and certain woodpeckers, clearly understand the message of chickadee high *zee* notes and will either freeze on the spot or dive for cover when they hear it. The pitch of this call may vary with the type of predator and may even give some indication of how dangerous the threat might be.

Another chickadee behavior is mobbing, which involves calling loudly and flying around very close to a stationary predator. Usually more than one chickadee is involved. Chickadees may mob predators at any time of year, although they do most of their mobbing in mid to late summer. Mobbing behavior can serve two functions. Summer mobbing by adult chickadees may serve to teach their offspring what kinds of creatures should be regarded as dangerous, before the family flock breaks up and the young chickadees set out to fend for themselves. In addition, mobbing itself, at any time of year, may sometimes succeed in persuading a predator to move away in search of a quieter, more peaceful place to live.

The *chick-a-dee-dee* call is one of the most interesting given by Black-capped Chickadees. In fact, it is called the *chick-a-dee* call complex, because there are so many versions of this call and they serve so many different functions. Unlike some of the calls described above, this one is given regularly, by either sex, at any time of year.

One fascinating thing about the *dee* notes of every chickadee, such as the three flockmates shown here, is that when a group of Black-capped Chickadees lives together for a while, certain qualities of their *dee* notes will converge on a common pattern. Therefore, the *dee* notes of every chickadee contain information about which flock it belongs to. It turns out that what we call the *chick-a-dee* call actually contains four note types—three associated with the part of the call we generally hear as *chick-a,* and the fourth being the familiar *dee* note. Studies suggest that the proportion of each note type within a *chick-a-dee* call could encode information about what the caller is most likely to do next.

When a chickadee hears a *chick-a-dee* call, how it responds may depend on context, rate, volume, proportion and sequence of note types, and perhaps several other factors we have not yet figured out. Certainly *chick-a-dee* calls can carry a bewildering variety of different messages. When a chickadee discovers a particularly rich food source, it may give a version of this call, which brings over its mate (in summer) or flockmates (in winter). If a chickadee gets separated from others, it may give this call; the answers help the birds get together again. After serious danger has passed, the *chick-a-dee* call, usually given by the highest-ranked bird present, serves as an all-clear signal to any other chickadees nearby. And finally, a long string of *dee* notes is often given as a scold note by chickadees in mildly dangerous situations, such as when they are safely up in a tree and see a cat on the lawn below.

After their offspring have become independent and have dispersed from their natal territory, adult chickadees undergo the post-breeding molt, in which they replace all of their feathers. Molting adults are very quiet and may be rather hard for humans to find, but their social behavior is still extremely important, because at this point the winter flocks are beginning to form. Adults that have lost their mates over the summer will choose or accept new ones; any summer floaters that did not get mates over the summer will also choose or accept them now. Sometimes these new pairs are made up of two older birds, usually as the result of summer mortality of one or both of their mates. The rest of the flock will be made up of chickadees fledged just a few weeks before and newly settled into the area.

Each chickadee that joins a flock as it forms in late summer or early fall must not only choose a mate, but also establish its own position within the flock's peck order. Each bird attempts to obtain the highest possible rank, often with a great deal of calling and posturing. Perhaps the most common visual display in these autumn aggressive encounters is body ruffling, which can be given by either sex but is most frequently given by young males. Body ruffling seldom lasts more than a split second and is often accompanied by gargle notes. This display, which can also be given at other times of year, always signals a high level of aggression.

In the display known as the ruffled crown, all of the feathers on top of the head are raised to their full height. This display typically indicates a sudden brief increase in aggressive tendencies and is often given when another chickadee of similar or lower rank approaches.

Another common, if brief, aggressive display is the gape, in which the displaying bird usually leans toward a rival and opens its bill several times in a row. Both of these displays indicate high aggression and may be accompanied by gargle notes. Ruffled crown displays and gapes are frequently given during flock formation but remain relatively common throughout the year.

Still another brief aggressive display is the bill-up, in which the displaying chickadee swings back its head so that its bill points straight up in the air. Bill-ups can be seen throughout the year but are perhaps most common during the spring when breeding territories are being established. Although this display indicates a high aggressive tendency, it may also signal some fear. It is given primarily in encounters between two fairly evenly matched birds.

Not all chickadee displays signal the likelihood of attack. General sleeking is a display given by chickadees in the presence of higher-ranking birds. It signals that the bird is not a threat to the other individual and helps prevent the displayer from being attacked. Posture is important here; the chickadee is not perched in the ordinary upright position, helping to convey the message that it is unlikely to attack.

The single wing-flick is a display in which the chickadee suddenly flashes out just one wing. This is an extremely brief display that is given primarily by chickadees suddenly confronted by more powerful individuals—either higher-ranked chickadees or members of larger species, such as a Song Sparrow.

Ballet is a prolonged and complex display that is particularly important in late summer and early fall during the process of establishing ranks within the newly forming flocks. This display involves a whole series of moves and countermoves, with changes in relative orientation between the contestants being of great importance. Generally, after the ballet has gone on for a while, the lower-ranked individuals will be the chickadees that face away from their rivals more,

whereas the higher-ranked birds (or winners in this encounter) will be those that face their rivals more directly. It is difficult to tell which of the chickadees in this picture is the higher-ranked bird. The chickadee near the bottom of the feeder is leaning away from the upper bird, which suggests that it is lower ranked, although its head position might indicate otherwise. One would have to watch the full progress of many such displays between the two individuals to determine which is the higher-ranked bird.

Accompanying the postural displays, more subtle facial expressions may also be extremely important in chickadee communication. In these four pictures of Black-capped Chickadees, taken under similar light conditions and with essentially the same background, the facial expressions, combined with body posture, each give a quite different message. The top left picture shows a chickadee's posture and expression when the bird is neither threatened nor threatening. The top right shows a chickadee that indicates some level of insecurity, with general sleeking, complete with flattened crown, and with the weight back such that the body is relatively vertical. Note that the line separating the white cheeks from the crown goes pretty much straight back as in the first picture. Yet this chickadee is clearly threatened by something, and its posture indicates that it will not threaten back. The bottom left picture shows a much more aggressive chickadee, with more horizontal posture and raised crown feathers. Note that the hind end of the cheeks is somewhat higher than the front end, so that the line separating crown from cheeks is no longer straight. The curve of this line in the bottom right picture is particularly strong. This likely indicates a somewhat increased level of tension. The precise meaning of a lot of these subtle facial expressions has yet to be worked out in Black-capped Chickadees. More studies, particularly of flock behavior, are needed in order to increase our understanding in this area.

6

Surviving the Cold of Winter

Winter can be a remarkably tough time for chickadees. The cold temperatures pose an obvious problem: chickadees are warm-blooded, and it costs a great deal of energy to maintain their body temperature so much higher than the surrounding air. In addition, there are fewer daylight hours in winter than at any other time of year. Yet chickadees need at least some daylight in which to forage. This means that the time when chickadees need the most food to withstand cold temperatures is precisely when they have the least time available to forage for that food. Add to this the fact that food levels available to chickadees are usually lower at this time of year, and you get some idea of the difficulties chickadees must overcome each winter.

The lack of daylight foraging time can be severe indeed. Near the northernmost part of the Black-capped Chickadee's range, in places like Fairbanks, Alaska, daylight in late December lasts just over four hours—very little time for the resident chickadees to get sufficient food to fuel a fasting period of almost twenty hours. Yet somehow the chickadees do manage to survive.

One adaptation that helps make survival possible is the timing of the daily activity period. During the shortest days of the year, chickadees start and end their activities at lower light levels than at any other time of year, thus maximizing the precious time available for foraging.

Another adaptation is the timing of the molt. Chickadees replace all of their feathers right after they finish breeding—the last possible period of high food resources and warm weather, before temperatures begin to drop as winter approaches. This means that the feathers are relatively new and thick right when chickadees need insulation the most.

Associated with this is the fact that chickadees, like other birds, can control the position of each of their contour feathers. When a chickadee is cold, it will fluff out its feathers, thus increasing the thickness—and consequently the insulation—of their coats. Since the body feathers are curved, they can be erected to a considerable extent yet still maintain their overlap with the adjacent feathers, thus holding in the warmth. The efficiency of this insulation in chickadees can be absolutely amazing—the difference between the temperature on the outer surface of the feathers and the skin temperature, only a half inch or so away, can be more than 70 Fahrenheit degrees (40 Celsius degrees).

In frigid weather, a chickadee's feet may need to be warmed up from time to time. Thus, on very cold days, chickadees often perch on just one foot, letting the other one thaw out up inside the breast feathers. After a while, the chickadee will change feet so that the other one can warm up as well. If the bird is startled in any way, the foot being warmed will come down instantly, because chickadees usually need to spring from both feet at once in order to take flight.

The ability of Black-capped Chickadees to fly long distances may have been compromised in a trade-off for extra protection against the cold. In very small birds like chickadees, there are some extra constraints on how dense a coat of feathers can be and still maintain aerodynamic properties—that is, in small birds, the thicker the coat of feathers, beyond a certain point, the less well they can fly long distances. Chickadees do have unusually dense plumage for their size, and they are notoriously poor distance fliers as well.

The nostrils of chickadees—near the base of the upper part of the bill—are covered with feathers. This is thought to help conserve some of the heat and moisture that would otherwise be lost as the bird breathes. Most birds lack this adaptation, but ravens and many of their relatives, which also spend winters in very cold areas, have feathered nostrils as well.

In order to survive the long, cold winter nights, each chickadee must find a suitable place to sleep. Particularly in cold weather, chickadees virtually always roost in enclosed places—either in dense vegetation or, when available, in cavities. The shelter of this cavity will provide the chickadee with protection from wind and snow. Perhaps the reason this chickadee is visiting its roost site in the middle of the day is to store a seed inside, ready to eat first thing in the morning.

The tail feathers of this chickadee were undoubtedly bent by spending the previous night in the cramped quarters of a winter roost cavity. After a bitter cold night, most members of a chickadee flock may have such curves in their tail feathers. This is because a typical winter roost cavity tends to be small—often quite a bit smaller than an ordinary nest cavity. The advantage of selecting smaller sites is that it takes less body heat to warm up the enclosed air.

Certain kinds of parids, including the Boreal Chickadee, may, on cold winter nights, actually roost in holes in the snow. Evidently they plunge into a deep snowbank, often at an angle, then dig a burrow several inches long. Since undisturbed snowbanks always contain a lot of trapped air, snow can provide excellent insulation. Once a chickadee has dug such a burrow, it may return to roost there regularly. Conceivably, Black-capped Chickadees could also use such snow roosts in situations where the snow is deep enough for burrows to be constructed.

This chickadee, taking a quick nap during the day, shows some indication of the typical roosting posture used each night: the chickadee's head is turned back over its shoulder, such that the scapular feathers partially cover its face. When roosting at night, the entire face is usually covered. This posture is an important heat-conserving adaptation; studies show that most of the heat loss from a chickadee's body is from the face region, especially the eyes. By covering this critical area with feathers, this potential heat loss is minimized. Each chickadee probably roosts alone; there is as yet no direct evidence that chickadees ever roost huddled together, although some related species, such as the Common Bushtit, are known to do so. Ordinarily, all the members of a winter flock will roost within that flock's range, and usually the roost sites will be fairly close together.

During the cold of winter, many seed-eating finches that stay north all winter typically deposit thick layers of fat just under their skin. This gives them a store of energy to be used in times when they cannot eat, such as during the long, dark northern winter nights. It may also increase their insulation against the cold. Wintering chickadees also store some fat under their skin, the amount being greatest just before they go to roost each night. Chickadees rarely put on the quantities of fat that juncos and other finches do, however; with their winter diet of half plant, half animal matter, they simply don't take in enough fat to be able to do so.

This presents a serious problem; with so little fat reserves, how can a tiny, warm-blooded bird like the chickadee have the energy necessary to survive until daybreak? The answer is truly amazing. On cold winter nights, chickadees go into regulated hypothermia, actually lowering their body temperature, in a controlled manner, down to about 12 or 15 Fahrenheit degrees (7 or 8 Celsius degrees) below their normal daytime temperature. This remarkable adaptation allows them to save enormous amounts of energy. When the outside temperature

is at the freezing point, hypothermia reduces a chickadee's hourly metabolic expenditures by almost 25 percent, and as the outside temperature gets even lower, the energy savings through hypothermia increase. Chickadees lower their body temperature by reducing the amount of shivering they do. Shivering generates heat through muscular work; thus when a chickadee gradually reduces its shivering, its body temperature will fall. Chickadees never let their temperature get low enough to affect their ability to escape danger, however. Even when they are in hypothermia, they can still fly.

At the approach of a storm, even though it won't arrive for several hours, chickadee feeding activity becomes much more intense. Even before humans can detect signs of an approaching storm, chickadee behavior indicates that they can tell when one is coming. Most birds have a special middle-ear receptor called the Vitali organ, which can sense incredibly small changes in barometric pressure. Pigeons, for example, can detect barometric changes between the air pressure at the floor and at the ceiling of an ordinary room. This special sensitivity permits birds to sense approaching storms and take appropriate action long before clouds appear or temperatures begin to drop.

Even so, winter storms can be hard on small birds like chickadees. In severe weather, chickadees usually restrict their activities greatly and fly as little as possible. Even in the best of conditions, flight can increase heat loss. The feathers below the wing are far less dense than in most other areas of the body, so in very cold weather, even short flights can drain a lot of heat from a chickadee.

During storms, chickadees usually spend much of their time near high concentrations of food such as feeders, especially if these are in sheltered areas. It also helps if they are near patches of dense vegetation that give protection from the wind. At times like these, the food chickadees have stored earlier in the fall can be critically important, potentially making the difference between death and survival.

Perhaps ice storms are the worst. When tree branches are all sheathed with ice, food items on the bark, such as insect eggs and pupae, are far harder to get at. Chickadees may be able to pound off some of the ice, but this uses up a lot of energy. If this ice melts soon, the effects won't be so bad, but if an ice storm is followed by a prolonged cold spell, chickadees may have a hard time of it. Big coniferous trees can provide something of a refuge. Their inner cones usually escape the ice coating, and the enclosed seeds may help the chickadees get through the worst of the storm.

Black-capped Chickadees have a wonderful assortment of adaptations for the winter: carefully hidden food items, dense winter coats, specially selected winter roost cavities, and, perhaps most remarkable of all, the ability to go into nightly hypothermia, thus conserving large amounts of energy and greatly increasing the chances of survival. No wonder they manage so well in places where few other small birds remain through the cold winter months.

Population Ecology

Many ecological factors affect the daily lives of Black-capped Chickadees—predation, starvation, competition both within and between species, and seasonal stresses such as winter's cold and the energy drain of reproduction. As soon as a young chickadee disperses from its native territory and sets out on its own, it must face and overcome ecological obstacles to survive.

It is late summer. This young chickadee has just dispersed, settled into a new area, and joined a newly forming local flock. Only a small proportion of its brothers and sisters will be lucky enough to make it that far. Exactly what happens to these young birds is very difficult to pinpoint. By counting how many young leave the nests in a certain area, we know approximately how many should be available to join flocks, assuming that about the same number will disperse into the area as disperse out, once they are independent. Yet year after year, virtually everywhere, more young chickadees leave nests than settle into local winter flocks, indicating that many die relatively soon after fledging. Some may simply starve— foraging takes practice, and some evidently don't learn all that rapidly. Others are undoubtedly taken by predators. Juvenile dispersal forces young chickadees to pass through unfamiliar areas where they do not

know local escape routes. The lucky ones will survive long enough to join winter flocks. Then they can learn all the safe spots and rich food sources in their new home range.

Even after a young chickadee has settled into a flock and learned about the flock range, it is not completely safe from predators. The Sharp-shinned Hawk eats mostly small birds, and its range largely overlaps that of Black-capped Chickadees, although in winter it is more prevalent in the southern part of the chickadee's geographic range. In many areas, Sharp-shinned Hawks are the most dangerous and effective predator that chickadees must face.

Chickadee populations that live too far north to overlap with Sharp-shinned Hawks in winter are still not safe, however, since they live within the range of the Northern Shrike. Northern Shrikes are not quite such bird specialists as Sharp-shinned Hawks; indeed, many seem to prefer eating small mammals when available. They do, however, sometimes eat small birds, including chickadees when they can catch them. When a shrike catches something too big to swallow whole, such as a chickadee, it kills it first, then often impales it on a sharp object such as a thorn. This is because shrikes lack strong talons like those of hawks and owls to hold down their prey. Once its prey is anchored on a thorn, the shrike can pull off pieces small enough to swallow.

Just how many young chickadees will settle into a winter flock in a given year? One factor that affects this number is how well adult chickadees survived during the past summer; the more older birds still alive at the end of the summer, the fewer vacancies available for young birds to fill in the newly forming flocks. A second factor is nesting success; in years when fewer young chickadees are produced, fewer will be available to join flocks in the fall.

The number of young birds settling in the fall into local winter flocks, at least in some areas, is significantly correlated to chickadee mortality later that winter. In autumns that lead to winters of low chickadee mortality, significantly more chickadees join local flocks than they do in falls leading to winters of higher mortality. In other words, chickadees actually seem to be able to predict how well they will survive in a given area during the coming winter, and adjust how many settle accordingly. Such predictions are likely based on the local food, such as the quantity of seed crops and possibly insect damage, which chickadees may use to assess how many eggs, pupae, or other stages will be available in the winter on the bark of local trees. As yet, it is not known which birds decide how many new recruits will join a flock in the fall—whether young chickadees decide to settle in areas where they see plenty of food, or whether the older birds permit more young chickadees to become members of their flocks when there are higher resource levels.

Young chickadees, when they join their first winter flock, must establish their place within the flock's peck order. The position each manages to get will have a considerable influence on how well it survives the winter. Relative rank can affect survival in several ways. For example, dominant chickadees get to feed in the safest and richest sites, while lower-ranked chickadees must search for food elsewhere. The fact that the subordinates are actually forced to feed in poorer locations by dominants' behavior has been clearly shown by removal experiments. This high-ranked male was removed from his flock and kept in an aviary for a few days. During his absence, lower-ranked chickadees instantly changed their behavior and started foraging in places where normally only he would be. After he was released, he took over the best spots, forcing the subordinates to go back to their former less favorable foraging sites.

Suppose a predator such as a Sharp-shinned Hawk flies over a chickadee flock coming in to a feeder. One or more members of the flock will give high-intensity alarm calls, and the chickadees will freeze instantly. After a while, the dominant member of the flock will give a *chick-a-dee* call, signaling that all is clear, and the flock members will start moving again. But that dominant bird is seldom the first one back to the feeder. Usually the first birds back to a feeder after an encounter with a predator are the lowest-ranked members of the flock. It is not known whether this is because of inexperience (low-ranking chickadees are often the young ones) or because subordinate birds, being forced to forage in poorer locations, are simply more hungry than the dominants. Whatever the reason, the first birds back to a feeder are at a greater risk because the predator may still be around.

Winter food levels themselves may also affect survival. Starvation can be a very real possibility. Levels of most kinds of foods often vary greatly from year to year. For the most part, in many areas, starvation may not be a big factor. Occasionally, however, during years of low natural food supply, periods of unusually cold weather will occur. This combination can be very hard on chickadees. In such years, the position a chickadee holds in the peck order again comes into play, and low-ranked chickadees, forced to look for food in inferior habitats, may well be the ones that do not make it.

When resources are in short supply, chickadees may have to compete for their share with members of other species. The effects of interspecific competition tend to be minimized by differences in foraging behavior. The chickadee's ability to hang from perches allows it to find food that less agile species might miss.

Very closely related species share the agility of the Black-capped Chickadee and potentially provide some of its most intense competition. In Europe, where flocks containing three, four, or even more parid species are relatively common, competition among them can be intense. In North America, however, the situation is quite different. First of all, overlap of geographic ranges here is minimal; over most of the Black-capped Chickadee's range, there are no other kinds of chickadees present. Where range overlaps do occur, habitat choices tend to minimize contact and competition. The typical habitat of Black-capped Chickadees is either deciduous or mixed (deciduous-coniferous) woodland. Of chickadee species whose range comes in contact with Black-capped Chickadees, only the Carolina Chickadee shares this habitat preference, and the range overlap between the two species is very small. Mountain, Boreal, and Chestnut-backed Chickadees all have at least some overlap with Black-capped Chickadees, but all three spend far more time foraging in coniferous forests than Black-capped Chickadees do. This minimizes competition, even where loose associations between two chickadee species occur.

Occasionally within the last half century or so, certain relatives of chickadees have undergone range extensions that increased their geographic overlap with Black-capped Chickadees. Chestnut-backed Chickadees have extended their range twice in this way. However, studies have shown that in each case, there were no adverse effects on Black-capped Chickadees.

Recently, Tufted Titmice have been extending their range northward in eastern North America, and this extension may be having some impact on Black-capped Chickadees. Certainly some short-term effects have been noted—the initial arrival of Tufted Titmice may be correlated at first with lowered Black-capped Chickadee population levels. But these effects may not last very long. One study noted a chickadee population decrease soon after the arrival of Tufted Titmice, but after a few years the chickadee numbers gradually increased until they regained their former levels. In my own study, I have noted what may be a more subtle effect of titmice on chickadee populations. About 1987–89, we had a sudden jump in local titmouse density. The major change in the local chickadee population seemed to be in the number of winter floaters. Up until this time, they had been exceptionally numerous, but similar floater densities have not shown up in any year after this increase in titmouse numbers.

Interspecific interactions can indeed be subtle. Wintering seedeaters like Common Redpolls that typically store a lot of fat under their skin can potentially become weighed down so that they are less mobile when a predator attacks. Chickadees, which carry far less subcutaneous fat, are a bit quicker and more maneuverable and thus have a better chance of escaping such an attack. This represents a trade-off. Birds like redpolls must have these fat reserves to keep them warm all night. By contrast, chickadees, which can go into hypothermia on cold nights, can afford to be lighter and thus are more able to dodge an attack.

Those chickadees that manage to avoid starvation, interspecific competition, and predator attacks will make it through the winter. At this point, a new challenge must be faced: every chickadee that survives the winter must compete with the rest for breeding territories and the chance to reproduce. These two chickadees and their mates are engaged in a typical spring boundary dispute. The severity of these disputes varies markedly from year to year. If factors such as predation or starvation have reduced the winter numbers sufficiently, there may be plenty of room for all surviving chickadees to breed. This sort of thing can happen anywhere, at least in some years. In much of the range of Black-capped Chickadees, however, the number surviving the winter in most years will exceed the number that can obtain local breeding territories, thus leading to fierce spring territorial battles.

This chickadee and his mate have succeeded in getting a breeding territory, but its quality is relatively poor. Their territory is in a built-up area, containing few potential nest sites, and the

cover is sparse and made up mostly of conifers, which tend to harbor less edible caterpillars than do deciduous trees. In regions where there is quite a bit of variation in habitat quality, such relatively poor areas may serve as buffer zones. In years when all of the chickadees that survive the winter can get breeding territories in the high-quality areas, chickadees may not even attempt to breed in the inferior habitat. In years when there are surplus chickadees at the end of the winter, however, those that do not make it in the superior habitat may attempt to breed in the poorer areas. Thus the breeding population in the good habitat stays relatively stable from year to year, while in poorer habitat breeding density may show quite large yearly fluctuations.

Breeding itself can be very hard on chickadees, particularly young females. Among female breeders, most mortality occurs during the late summer and early fall of their first breeding season. Two factors seem to contribute to this mortality. One is the initial rank of the female when she joined her first flock the previous fall: females who ranked relatively high during the winter have a much better chance of surviving the following breeding season. The other is the relative experience of her mate: females mated to older, experienced males survive their first breeding season significantly better than do females mated to inexperienced males. Older, experienced males probably provide more food in courtship feeding, which may be crucial to female condition during egg laying and incubation. They also may be able to provide better help in protecting the nest. Predators such as snakes, weasels, squirrels, and raccoons all may attack chickadee nests, and often the male and female cooperate in their displays to either attack or lure away such dangers.

Perhaps the most unexpected threat to breeder female chickadees and their nests is the innocent-looking House Wren. In some areas, these wrens often destroy more chickadee nests than do any of the predators mentioned. The wrens, which also nest in cavities, attempt to take over every potential nest site within their own breeding territory, regardless of who has been using it. House Wrens may enter a chickadee nest, pierce all the eggs, then remove the remains, along with a quantity of nesting material. They are also known to kill nestling chickadees, and they may even attack incubating females. After a successful attack, the invading House Wren typically fills the nest cavity with material of its own. In one study done in eastern Massachusetts, 20 percent of the Black-capped Chickadee nests were destroyed by House Wrens.

Brown-headed Cowbirds often lay their eggs in nests of birds the size of Black-capped Chickadees. They seldom parasitize chickadees in this way, however, primarily because chickadees nest in cavities. Most chickadee nests like this one have entrances that are simply too small for cowbirds to enter.

Average life expectancies for Black-capped Chickadees are not very high; even for young chickadees that have fledged, dispersed, and settled into their first winter flocks, the average life span is just over a year. But for those chickadees that make it through their first winter and manage to get breeding territories the following spring, the average life span is somewhat higher—often three years or more, depending on the area. And yet a few particularly hardy chickadees may live and breed for more than ten years! Given the everyday hazards of chickadee life, these must be wise birds indeed.

Relations with Humans

People who have chickadees living nearby are very lucky; chickadees are a real joy to have around. Unfortunately, not all locations are suitable for chickadees. Some city areas are so built up that they don't contain enough trees for chickadees to live in. Trees are essential for several reasons. In summer, their leaves can host caterpillars that are necessary for food. In winter, insects and spiders can be found hidden on and under their bark. The seeds of some trees often serve as important winter food for chickadees. Trees can provide cover from wind, places to hide from predators, safe roosting sites, and places in which to nest. Clearly, without a certain number of trees in the area, there is little chance of attracting chickadees.

In areas with sufficient trees, chickadees can easily be attracted to feeders, especially in winter. Sunflower seeds are by far the most widely used seed for stocking feeders in most areas, but chickadees will also come to feeders containing other kinds of seed, and some individuals can develop a decided liking for the more expensive varieties, such as thistle seeds. Seed mixes, which typically contain a large amount of hard yellowish millet, will attract more kinds of birds; here chickadees will tend to pick out the sunflower seeds and ignore the rest.

An almost endless variety of feeders are available. Some of the more costly ones are designed to be squirrelproof, and many of these are quite effective. If you have enough trees, however, you may want to try a less expensive method of squirrelproofing. Tie a rope to two trees about 20 feet above the ground. Then attach one end of a second rope to the first one halfway between the two trees. Hang an inexpensive tube feeder from the second rope. Keep the feeder at least four feet from the ground and from any tree, and it will be relatively safe from squirrels.

Suet feeders are also very effective at bringing in chickadees. The colder the weather, the more attractive suet is to the birds. Chickadees, titmice, nuthatches, and woodpeckers all crowd to suet feeders on cold winter days. Squirrels, raccoons, and opossums may also try to get at your suet. The most effective defense against these mammals is to enclose the suet in wire mesh. Half- or quarter-inch hardware cloth works fine, provided it is wired together very carefully; raccoons, in particular, are highly intelligent and have remarkably nimble fingers.

Before setting up feeders, give some thought to their location. Select feeder sites so as to minimize danger to the birds. All too often chickadees die by crashing into windows while carrying off a seed from a feeder. One way to reduce this risk is to mount a feeder right on the window. Birds that come to such a feeder run little risk of banging into the glass because they

are so close when they land and take off. Other ways to help avoid this problem include putting hawk-shaped silhouettes on the windows or keeping screens year-round on all windows close to feeders. Do not place feeders near low, thick cover where cats can hide, and never place low feeders close to roads, as this will greatly increase the birds' chances of being hit by cars.

Some people question the value of feeders. A few suggest that the birds attracted to feeders may be convenient concentrations of food for predators like hawks or shrikes. One way to minimize this danger is to provide cover close by where chickadees can hide, so long as the cover is well up above the ground so that cats cannot use it to lie in ambush.

Studies have clearly shown that supplementary food from feeders can increase chickadee overwinter survival. Moreover, chickadees that have access to feeders have just as much success at finding and handling natural foods as do those that have never used feeders. In other words, Black-capped Chickadees are not made dependent by the presence of feeders.

Another good way to attract chickadees to your yard is to provide them with water for drinking and bathing. Hanging containers are particularly effective, and somewhat safer from predators than birdbaths at ground level.

You can plan your garden and landscaping to increase its attractiveness to chickadees. Include food plants such as sunflowers and various berries. Some of the chickadees' favorite insect foods are found mostly on deciduous trees like oaks and maples. Evergreen trees and shrubs will provide shelter, and the seeds of many conifers may also provide good sources of winter food.

Providing food, water, and shelter will attract chickadees, but if there are no available nest sites, the local chickadees will still be forced to leave in the spring. Putting up nest boxes can be particularly effective in suburban settings, where natural nest sites are often rare. Entrances should be 1 $\frac{1}{8}$ inches in diameter and at least 6 inches above the floor of the box. Chickadee houses may be attached to a tree, anywhere from 7 to 12 feet up, usually just below the level of the lowest branches. Filling the boxes about a one-third full of coarse sawdust will give the chickadees something to excavate; opinions differ as to whether this makes the boxes more attractive to chickadees. Most boxes are made of wood, though recently researchers have made nest boxes for chickadees out of sections of PVC piping; these have reportedly been very successful.

As human populations expand and woodland dwindles, how will this affect chickadees? Obviously, clear-cutting, especially on a large scale, will be disastrous. Under some circumstances, however, smaller-scale logging can actually have positive effects. This is because the Black-capped Chickadee is an edge species, their best habitat, at least during the breeding season, being the edges of woodland. A patchwork of small blocks of woodland is thus potentially better for chickadees than the same total area of woods concentrated into a single large area.

Black-capped Chickadees are among the most wonderful and intriguing birds one can ever encounter. They are extremely attractive and endlessly fascinating.

Although we have learned a great deal about the natural history of Black-capped Chickadees, a lot still awaits discovery. In many cases, all that is required is a good pair of binoculars, an inquiring mind, and plenty of patience. It is my hope that some of you will go out and make a few of these discoveries for yourselves.

Photo Credits

Page 1
Bill Marchel

Page 2
John Heidecker (top)
R. Cartmell/VIREO
(bottom)

Page 3
Robert McCaw

Page 4
Bill Marchel (top)
Bill Marchel (bottom)

Page 5
V. Hasselblad/VIREO

Page 6
Richard Day/Daybreak
Imagery (left)
Doug Locke (right)

Page 7
B. Randall/VIREO (top)
Rob Curtis/VIREO (bot-
tom)

Page 8
Tom Vezo

Page 9
Russell Hansen (top)
Gary W. Carter (center)
Russell Hansen (bot-
tom)

Page 10
Robert McCaw

Page 11
Susan Smith (top)
Jim Yuskavitch (bot-
tom)

Page 12
Stephen B. Antus, Jr.

Page 13
Susan Smith

Page 14
Robert McCaw (top)
Bill Marchel (bottom)

Page 15
Robert McCaw (top)
Gregory K. Scott (bot-
tom)

Page 16
Gary W. Carter (top)
Ron Morreim (center)
Bill Marchel (bottom)

Page 17
Jim Yuskavitch (top)
Stephen B. Antus, Jr.
(center)
Stephen B. Antus, Jr.
(bottom)

Page 18
Stephen B. Antus, Jr.
(top)
D. Dvorak, Jr. (center)
Richard Day/Daybreak
Imagery (bottom)

Page 19
Jim Yuskavitch (top)
Gary W. Carter (center)
Robert McCaw (bottom)

Page 20
Doug Locke

Page 21
Gregory K. Scott (top)
Ned Smith/VIREO (bot-
tom)

Page 22
Robert McCaw

Page 23
Gary W. Carter (top)
Jim Yuskavitch (bot-
tom)

Page 24
Gary W. Carter (top)
Jim Yuskavitch (bot-
tom)

Page 25
James D. Young/VIREO
(top)
R. & N. Bowers/VIREO
(center)
Jim Roetzel (bottom)

Page 26
Russell C. Hansen (top)
Gary W. Carter (bottom)

Page 27
Leonard Lee Rue III
(top)
Ron Morreim (bottom)

Page 28
Susan Smith

Page 29
Susan Smith (top)
Susan Smith (bottom)

Page 30
Susan Smith (top)
Gary W. Carter (center)
Bill Marchel (bottom)

Page 31
Gregory K. Scott (top)
Robert McCaw (bottom)

Page 32
Bill Marchel (top)
Susan Smith (center)
Leonard Lee Rue III
(bottom)

Page 33
Jim Roetzel (top)
Robert McCaw (bottom)

Page 34
Ron Morreim (top)
Tom Vezo (bottom)

Page 35
Bill Marchel

Page 36
Susan Smith

Page 37
Ron Morreim (top)
Bill Marchel (bottom)

Page 38
Marie Read

Page 39
Marie Read (top)
Robert McCaw (bottom)

Page 40
Gregory K. Scott (top)
Tom Vezo (center)
Gregory K. Scott (bot-
tom)

Page 41
Doug Locke (top)
Richard Day/Daybreak
Imagery (center)
Susan Smith(bottom)

Page 42
Gary W. Carter (top)
D. Dvorak Jr. (center)
Leonard Lee Rue III
(bottom)

Page 43
Bill Marchel (top)
Tom Vezo (bottom)

Page 44
Stephen B. Antus, Jr.
(top)
Stephen B. Antus, Jr.
(center)
Gregory K. Scott (bottom)

Page 45
Gary W. Carter (top)
Gary W. Carter (center)
Tom Vezo (bottom)

Page 46
Gary W. Carter (top)
Stephen B. Antus, Jr.
(bottom)

Page 47
Gary W. Carter

Page 48
John Serrao

Page 49
Susan Smith (top)
Stephen B. Antus, Jr.
(bottom)

Page 50
Susan Smith

Page 51
Robert McCaw (top)
Robert McCaw (center)
Susan Smith (bottom)

Page 52
Doug Locke (top)
Robert McCaw (bottom)

Page 53
Richard Day/Daybreak
Imagery (top)
Robert McCaw (bottom)

Page 54
Jim Yuskavitch (top)
John Heidecker (bottom)

Page 55
Richard Day/Daybreak
Imagery (top)
Ron Morreim (center)
Russell C. Hansen (bottom)

Page 56
Jim Roetzel (top)
Robert McCaw (bottom
left)
Robert McCaw (bottom
right)

Page 57
Leonard Lee Rue III
(top)
Susan Smith (center)
Leonard Lee Rue III
(bottom)

Page 58
D. Dvorak, Jr. (top)
Tom Vezo (bottom)

Page 59
Tom Vezo

Page 60
Steve Maslowski

Page 61
Doug Locke (top)
Robert McCaw (bottom)

Page 62
Tom Vezo (top)
Susan Smith (bottom)

Page 63
Tom Vezo (top left)
Tom Vezo (top right)
Tom Vezo (bottom left)
Tom Vezo (bottom right)

Page 64
Bill Marchel

Page 65
Robert McCaw (top)
Ron Morreim (center)
Tom Vezo (bottom)

Page 66
Bill Marchel (top)
Bill Marchel (bottom)

Page 67
Russell C. Hansen (top)
Gregory K. Scott (bottom)

Page 68
Robert McCaw (top)
Susan Smith (bottom)

Page 69
D. Dvorak, Jr. (top)
Robert McCaw (bottom)

Page 70
Susan Smith (top)
C.H. Greenewalt/
VIREO (center)
D. Dvorak, Jr. (bottom)

Page 71
Gary W. Carter

Page 72
Stephen B. Antus, Jr.

Page 73
Leonard Lee Rue III
(top)
Robert McCaw (bottom)

Page 74
Stephen B. Antus, Jr.

Page 75
Tom Vezo (top)
Leonard Lee Rue III
(bottom)

Page 76
Robert McCaw (top)
Stephen B. Antus, Jr.
(bottom)

Page 77
B. Small/VIREO

Page 78
Robert McCaw (top)
Susan Smith (center)
Gary W. Carter (bottom)

Page 79
Gregory K. Scott

Page 80
Jim Yuskavitch (top)
John Heidecker (bottom)

Page 81
Tom Vezo

Page 82
Susan Smith (top)
Susan Smith (bottom)

Page 83
Gregory K. Scott (top)
Robert McCaw (bottom)

Page 84
Tom Vezo (top)
Tom Vezo (bottom)

Page 85
Todd Fink/Daybreak
Imagery (top)
Tom Vezo (bottom)

Page 86
Bill Marchel (top)
Bill Marchel (bottom)

Selected References

Barnea, A., and F. Nottebohm. 1994. Seasonal recruitment of hippocampal neurons in adult free-ranging Black-capped Chickadees. *Proceedings of the National Academy of Science* 91:11217-21.

Brittingham, M. C., and S. A. Temple. 1992. Does winter bird feeding promote dependency? *Journal of Field Ornithology* 63:190-94.

Clemmons, J. R., and M. M. Lambrechts. 1992. The waving display and other nest site anti-predator behavior of the Black-capped Chickadee. *Wilson Bulletin* 104:749-56.

Clemmons, J. R. 1995. Vocalizations and other stimuli that elicit gaping in nestling Black-capped Chickadees *(Parus atricapillus)*. *Auk* 112:603-12.

Cooper, S. J., and D. L. Swanson. 1994. Seasonal acclimitization of thermoregulation in the Black-capped Chickadee. *Condor* 96:638-46.

Ficken, M. S., and J. W. Popp. 1992. Syntactical organization of the gargle vocalization of the Black-capped Chickadee, *Parus atricapillus*. *Ethology* 91:156-68.

Gill, F. B., A. M. Mostrom, and A. L. Mack. 1993. Speciation in North American chickadees: I. Patterns of mtDNA genetic divergence. *Evolution* 47:195-212.

Grubb, T. C., Jr., and C. L. Bronson. 1995. Artificial snags as nesting sites for chickadees. *Condor* 97:1067-70.

Herz, R. S., L. Zanette, and D. F. Sherry. 1994. Spatial cues for cache retrieval by Black-capped Chickadees. *Animal Behaviour* 48:343-51.

Karosov, W. H., M. C. Brittingham, and S. A. Temple. 1992. Daily energy and expenditure by Black-capped Chickadees *(Parus atricapillus)* in winter. *Auk* 109:393-95.

Otter, K., L. Ratcliffe, and P. T. Boag. 1994. Extra-pair paternity in the Black-capped Chickadee. *Condor* 96:218-22.

Piaskowski, V. D., C. M. Weise, and M. S. Ficken. 1991. The body ruffling display of the Black-capped Chickadee. *Wilson Bulletin* 103:426-34.

Shackleton, S. A., and L. Ratcliffe. 1994. Matched and counter-singing signals escalation of aggression in Black-capped Chickadees. *Ethology* 97:310-16.

Smith, S. M. 1991. *The Black-capped Chickadee and Related Species; Behavioral Ecology and Natural History*. Ithaca, NY: Cornell University Press.

Smith, S. M. 1993. The Black-capped Chickadee. In *The Birds of North America,* no. 39, edited by A. Poole, P. Stettenheim, and F. Gill. Philadelphia: The Academy of Natural Sciences; Washington, DC: The American Ornithologists' Union.

Smith, S. M. 1994. Social influences on the dynamics of a northeastern Black-capped Chickadee population. *Ecology* 75:2043-51.

Smith, S. M. 1995. Age-specific survival in breeding Black-capped Chickadees (*Parus atricapillus*). *Auk* 112:840-46.

Suhonen, J. 1993. Predation risk influences the use of foraging sites by tits. *Ecology* 74:1194-1203.

About the Author

Susan M. Smith, a member of the Department of Biological Sciences at Mount Holyoke College, is the author of *The Black-capped Chickadee and Related Species; Behavioral Ecology and Natural History.* She has also written numerous articles on chickadees and chickadee behavior for ornithological journals and birding magazines. She lives in South Hadley, Massachusetts.